facets of life

God Bless You!

"We choose the disposition we carry each day"

A Collection of POETRY, PROSE and PRAISE

RENNA I ROBERTS-GORE

FACETS OF LIFE

Published by Purposely Created Publishing Group™

Copyright © 2016 Renna Roberts-Gore

ALL RIGHTS RESERVED.

ISBN (ebook): 978-1-942838-73-9

ISBN (paperback): 978-1-942838-72-2

Printed in the United States of America

Dedication

To my mother, Avonelle—

who is probably sitting out on the verandah of her Caribbean home with her legs crossed, enjoying a beautiful breeze. Mom, you've always kept my awards for essays, papers and poems. You've always critiqued and praised my writing. You've always asked me, "When will you publish your book?" Well here you are—this is for you. Proudly, I give you my first of many books in dedication to you. Thank you for being the world's best mother. I love you.

Your Daughter Renna
"The Author" :)

Acknowledgements

My acknowledgements are straight to the heart of the matter. First I thank God for sustaining me, for quickening my thoughts and for ideas afresh for the duration of this project. To my husband who, with the patience of Job, dealt with every doubt and fear I had throughout my writing. I love you dearly.

I'll tell you a secret: you want everyone to love your work as much as you do. Releasing it to be published is like putting your little one on the school bus. I believe the first positive written review will be like hearing from the teacher that your child is fine.

To the world's most wonderful parents, Roosevelt and Avonelle Roberts, may your blessings be many, and may you live long in divine health to receive them all.

To my son, you will always be my inspiration.

To my younger brother, my only sibling, thank you for being the best ever. Love you.

To my dream of a publisher, Ms. Tieshena Davis, and to the entire capable and progressive staff of Purposely Created Publishing, I thank you for allowing me the chance to share my gift.

To all the naysayers, to everyone who told me "No"—THANK YOU! :)

To ME—You did it! Yes, you did the work Christ told you that you were born for.

Finally, to all my readers, please ENJOY your reading, and I thank you for allowing me into your hearts, homes and discussions. My prayer is that this work will have a positive impact on your lives going forward. This is just the first of many.

Introduction

Trust in the Lord with all thine heart; and lean not unto thine own understanding.

In all thy ways acknowledge him, and he shall direct thy paths.

Proverbs 3:5-6

I learned early, at the age of six, that the world would listen to you if you wrote well. As I got older, I realized that any emotion could be expressed in black and white and that words have no boundaries. Through the joy of reading, I discovered a world of beauty that shape-shifted to suit moods, atmosphere and circumstances. Through writing, I've allowed myself to be an emotional nudist/chameleon, baring all with no visit from the shame fairy.

The above is my absolute favorite scripture and motto for my life. Early on in my first career as an EMT, I hungered to write seriously. Educators, family and strangers told me that I had the gift of writing, but I disregarded those urgings with youthful foolishness. However, the thing that is your *gift* will chase you even in your dreams, until it is shared with the world so that it can make a difference. I've come to realize that the words we pen can heal. They can let someone know they are not alone and can reassure a person that "this too shall pass." Words can empower, guide, comfort, prepare for battle and end a recurring nightmare.

That brings me to my book that you are going to enjoy immensely and savor like the last piece of your favorite chocolate bar. *Facets Of Life: A Collection of Poetry, Prose and Praise* is a gathering of emotions and experiences that you are going to love. Take your time reading this gem, as you will run the full gamut of emotional expression and have a sense that you are able to move a mountain by the time you get to the end.

I wrote this book because I want to share my gift with my readers, and I am delighted to learn if you love this book as much as I loved putting it together. There are two older poems in this body of work, but the bulk was written over a six-month period (March–September 2015). I find inspiration in everything, and I sincerely feel that everyone over the age of 18 can identify with one or many of the topics presented.

I decided on poetry because it comes to me so easily and is so easily understood in so many different languages the world over. I am a Christian—a woman of strong faith—and you will come to find that out about me over time. I am not a one-trick pony! I promise to keep writing for you. But I can only know which ones are your favorites if you let me know in reviews. My personal favorites are all of them. I believe in this collection and love it dearly, and I am so excited about you reading it and recommending it to your friends and book clubs and even at tea in the afternoon when it gets chilly. Honestly though, if I had to pick a few that really stir me, they would be "Legacy," because of my deep love for my family, and "My Girdle Tried To Kill Me"—a hilarious piece of work that came to mind as I folded a foundation garment and stuck it in its drawer.

The statuses that I share from my personal Facebook page are thoughts that flowed directly from my spirit—what I am led to type on a particular day, I type. I have found that a few of them pair well with my poems, so I have grouped those together. Someone, somewhere may need that exact word, and as the spirit leads, I obey. There are so many times that I have received private messages from friends who described a current situation that a status update of mine addressed unknowingly. In moments like that I am humbled to a position of bended-knee.

I have asked the Lord to continue to use me, and I continually express to Him how blessed I am that He should find me a worthy vessel. It is through my cracks that my light shines. Think of yourselves as the most prized creation that's been tossed about, cracked and tried. Now think of your creator who loves you so much that he picks your pieces up and glues you back together by his grace. Your creation had its purpose in place long before you even knew yourself, long before you were a thought. Those cracks made you stronger, and since perfection in this realm is impossible to achieve, allow your light to come through in those tiny places that were intentionally left unsettled. When your crack is similar to mine, we are able to swap stories and know that we are not alone in this world.

Enjoy!

FACET

fac·et

ˈfasət/

noun

plural noun: facets

One side of something many-sided, especially of a cut gem.

synonyms: surface, face, side, plane

"the many facets of the gem"

A particular aspect or feature of something:

"participation by the laity in all facets of church life"

synonyms: aspect, feature, side, dimension, characteristic, detail, point, ingredient, strand.

Table of Contents

MY "JOURNEY-WOMAN'S" PRAYER

Dear Lord, help me to stay focused. When all Hell breaks loose, I know I'm on the right path. Help me keep my eyes fixed on you. Whenever I get weary, just blow on me. Help keep my gait sure; tighten the straps of my shoes. Busy foolishness elsewhere. I thank you for all you've done so far—especially those things I thought were impossible in my human way of thinking. Renew my energy and intellect for the rest of my journey. I know why you sent me here. I know I'm close to the place and purpose you anointed me for. Please continue to hide me under your wings from the things that seek to destroy me. All things work together for good for them that love you. I love you, and I know you love me too. Grant me the ability to look back and smile. Amen.

≈

LEGACY

My name shall not die with me
Forgotten, lost in Her-story
When they lay me down to rest,
My flesh alone shall die.

My name, unsure from whence it came
In all its splendor, shall remain
Its strength shall grace lips far and wide
Across the globe, it shall survive

We build or break our family names
We should ensure they do remain
If we knew the power names hold
We'd live more humbly—not quite so bold

Just what will you leave behind?
Will generations next be kind?
Are you paving the way for them?
How will you be remembered then?

This short time we spend on earth
Just how significant was your birth?
I cannot afford to see
My name being buried with me.

THIS BLOOD INSIDE ME

Through me flows the blood of slaves
Defiant and strong, silenced yet brave
My ancestors all never met, still they thrive
Their wisdom guides me, it helps keep me alive

Sometimes life may cut me like it cut through them
But their struggles I feel like a fire from within
My will is encouraged right through each storm
With my life their second chance is reborn

This time to right all those things that went wrong
This time to thrive, not to just "get along"
This time to purpose this blood loaned to me
This time our destiny's face to see

Please know the responsibility each person shares
Those who came before us tried their best to prepare
Through no fault of their own they were killed on the way
Now the burden falls on all of us to fix things this day

Though weary and lonely you feel, don't give in
To do so is just the most dangerous sin
Your future will search for that map in their blood
They'll need it to take them safely through the flood

Don't disappoint them!

MY MOTHER

Avonelle

A VAILABLE *she is to all who need her*

V IRTUOUS *no other can compare*

O RDAINED *to be the perfect wife and mother*

N URTURING *to all those in her care*

E DIFYING *just one purpose she is blessed with*

L OVING *born to be it, giving freely*

L OYAL ighting *silently in prayer*

E VERYTHING *is what she means to me*

MY FAMILY TREE

Hundreds of years ago, you were just a seed
Unsure if you would thrive they prayed you would
Now bold you stand apart from all around you
Providing shade you've done a world of good

Your leaves are lush, green, shiny—countless wonders
Those fallen ones they too have left their mark
Your branches strong, sustained in stormy weather
They couldn't know this at the very start

Beneath the ground your roots so strong and many
Spread far and wide so hidden from the sky
Yet if the tree cut down should be its portion
Those many roots so deep they shall survive

I dare to sit beneath you in your splendor
Not knowing all the things that gave you care
I shall water you when drought threatens to harm you
Just for the privilege of being rooted here.

∾

ANTIGUA, MY HOME SWEET HOME ❤

Island life is oh so sweet
She offers you a safe retreat
Warmth from the sun the whole year round
Whenever I miss her I am homeward bound

A beach for every day of the year
Yes! I have counted, and they are super clear
Whatever your palate you'll find the food you like
If your thing is alcohol you can find the perfect spike

It's our nature to be loving and to smile when greeting you
What we give to our people, we will give the same to you
Antigua is beautiful, majestic to her core
I promise if you visit her once, you will return for more

Every island is a gem in her own perfect right
But my island is the very best be it day or night.

Where land and sea make beauty...

෴

RICH HARVEST

For generations to come, even when the planting of the seed is long forgotten, the reaping shall continue. Never wonder why some folks just spin in circles; it is their destiny to do so. The seed was planted long before they started to spin. Be mindful of how you live, especially if you have children. Unconsciously, we pave the path our children take with our thoughts and actions. How can you say you love your children and treat somebody else's child badly? Did you forget they are someone's child too? How can you expect the plates of your children to be full when you feed no one else? We should think of ourselves as bits of energy. Good energy attracts like energy. Be good to people; when you do, you are actually being good to you and yours. God Bless!

HANDLE GOD'S ANOINTED...*GENTLY*

Be careful how you handle every person you should meet
Through business, on the telephone, walking down the street
Be kind and ever thoughtful; assist them in every way
If they carry God's anointing, they may save your life one day

They may be a drunk, a floozy, an opportunist thief
Or someone down on luck it seems, trying to make ends meet
Or they could be tagged "loser," poor without a home
The least important person does not walk this life alone

Sometimes they've lost everything, downtrodden and depressed
Their mess as bad as it may look is only just a test.
Father God has long anointed them in ways you'll never know
It's in the way you treat them your blessings start to show

Because they beg you on the corner without a bite to eat
This doesn't take away anointing placed from the mercy seat
One touch from God is all it takes to take that person far
Be kind to them, you just don't know—who they really are!

∽

HANDLING OTHERS

If you want to know how to handle somebody, ask the Lord. He may tell you to pray for them; he may guide the time and conversation you have with them, or how to give them what they need most at the time.

One thing is sure—whatever way he rests on your spirit will be beneficial to them and to you. It will help and not harm. Just think when you witness someone do harm, misuse, destroy another individual, they are an agent of the devil. God did not send that person, even if they said he did. He already has my number! Test any spirits who present themselves to you with the **power of prayer**!

∾

BLACK BEAUTY

From milky shades to those of midnight.
Royal blues and sun-kissed hues
Cinnamon toast, warm butter, perfectly baked brown.
These are the shades that make Black Beauty!
Unique blends of soil weaved through our flesh
Made in God's own image, then he smiled
Said, "It is good." Fearfully and wonderfully made
A friend of sunlight...
Hair like wool—just like King Jesus.
Full lips that bring new meaning to a kiss

Sturdy feet, broad hips to birth a nation
Manly, broad shoulders to carry each load
Just our skin, our stride implies durability
Just our voice commands a listening ear
With music in its chords our laugh a drumbeat
Feisty spirit born from those of old
My heart weeps though—
We do not know how powerful we are
If only we would stand together
Hold our heads high and walk into our purpose as One!

First though—if we could love our own selves
If we knew our black is beautiful
We'd love each other and know that every other shade of
Skin is beautiful too!

~

PREJUDICE

When we board a plane, we encounter all walks of life—every color of the rainbow. To get where we are going, we purchase a ticket and give absolutely no thought to who may be on the flight. The thing is, heaven will be like this, and so will hell. Both will be a mixed bag of souls. If you are black and can't stand white people, I've got news for you—heaven and hell will have white people too. If you are white and detest my black skin, whether you go up or down, black people will be present. How can you call yourself a Christian with unforgiveness, scorn, and unacceptance in your heart? Don't keep me in your heart and spoil your chances of entering heaven. Don't allow my appearance to offend you enough that you are distracted from Kingdom affairs that will benefit you. Don't focus on me when you should be working hard and miss out on the best retirement plan there is. Pretense gets us nowhere. Remember, God knows our hearts. *The whole of heaven is first class.* Jesus paid the price for me to travel in style on that trip. Will you be there? I really do hope so. All I can do is pray for you, but it's entirely up to you. I'll tell you this much, even if you don't come, I will be there!

IN THE HOOD

The hood has a smell, stays with you your whole lifetime
Despair, hunger, poverty and strife
Don't you look down your nose at me, "Sally from da Hood"
Not because you've "married up," now somebody's wife

Lest I remind you I remember you real well
Left your momma back here living in hell
That drug dealer turned you, promised sweet things
Straight out the hood you flew on them wings

I ain't mad at ya! Nah...I woulda left too
Your short memory shocks me, you don't have a clue
We need to look back from whence we came
Until we reach a hand back that smell will remain

Your momma didn't have much; still she gave so much
The kids knew after school she'd have something to eat
They'd all sit around her, do homework or play
Her warm meals and friendship kept many off the street

Now what will you do for the hood of your birth?
You may say you owe no one, but that's not how it works
I heard your dealer husband ate a bullet last week
Saw it on the news, finally caught up with his quirks

I hope you aren't hiding from his dangerous friends
We don't need any more trouble in "hell"
Hell can't be so bad because here you stand
I hope this time around you will lend us a hand

∾

SHADOWS

The funny thing about your shadow
Is that in the dark it leaves you
Yet trust we put in flesh like us
When betrayal comes we argue and fuss

If that shadow of ours changes shape
Sometimes it is hasty, no patience to wait
A mind of her own yet a friend since birth
Must we let a person's treatment determine our worth?

A forever friend, yet she laughs in the dark
A dancing, changing work of art
She waits with us wherever we are
Always close by, never very far
If my shadow changes her mind when she feels
Deserts me, or deciding my sins to reveal
How can I trust another human like me
Whose shadow has allowed me their dark side to see

∾

SUCH A WASTE OF TIME

So let me get this straight
I should wait…on you
Let's examine how long
I've waited already, shall we?
Ten years ago you said you'd leave
Give you some time, she was sick,
The boys needed you,
The dog had an appointment
The goldfish needed surgery
Ten years: 5 259 487.66 minutes
All that time little pieces of me have died
That time has been subtracted from my life
Once time is lost, you just can't get it back
Years of forgotten birthdays
Uncelebrated celebrations
Lonely holidays
Unaccompanied doctors visits
Unfertilized eggs
Grays in places I will not mention
Surprise pains and busted transmissions
Tortured nights of digital stimulation
Lines in my face that weren't there before
The furniture that was not bought
A home that I gave up
The bed whose left side remained firm
Winters with no warmth

Sunlight that just wasn't bright enough
…and me, I don't even know who I am anymore
But the person I am won't wait anymore
You were such a waste of time!

~

WHAT'S IN A KISS?

I can tell where you've been
By the taste of your breath
If you are sad or happy, worried or tense
Your kiss betrays you

Your eyes may not close completely
Your hands at my waist may not wrap me as sure
Your tongue may not offer its usual passion
Your kiss betrays you...

Your lips usually claim mine
Indecent and invasive
Our souls would touch in time gone by
But today, your kiss betrays you...

Your lips and mine had a dance going on
They spoke a language unknown even to us
Now the message yours speak mine can't understand
Your kiss betrays you...

I'm here for you as I normally am
Though your actions do not permit you to lean
Against the familiar lips that are mine
Your absent kiss betrays you...

~

THIS WORLD IS ROUND

I loved you a long time ago
Before I had the sense to know
That you would crumble up my heart
And spread its pieces all apart

If I had known you'd take my soul
Leave in its place a gaping hole
I would have turned the other way
Searched for love another day

If I had thought you'd take my fears
Displaying them like the cheapest wares
I would've never let you close to me
Or let all of my feelings free

I wonder do you sleep at night
Or do those eyes of yours put up a fight?
I bet that sleep just never wins
Since you've committed countless sins

I want to know what made you feel
My sanity was yours to steal?
Remember my dear stand firm on the ground
As you'll soon find out this world is round.

6/9/2003

∽

BLOOD SACRIFICE

Some sacrifice their children for wealth and fame
For promotion, recognition, material gain
They dabble with the devil to cancel out debt
But Jesus shed blood at Calvary this they forget

Young lives cut short for their parents to thrive
I wonder how they sleep at night, how do they survive?
Fake tears, fake time of mourning once the deed is done
Deaths unexplained—the devil's having fun

Give it some time, watch what springs from the ground
Beneath where that blood spilled, new life will be found
But God sees and knows every deal that we make
Success will be short-lived unless they awake

My eyes are wide open, I cannot be fooled
By salty tears and wet cheeks, re-read the "Golden Rule"

I won't accept L for 7 nor 6 for 9
I am one among many who refuse to be blind

Enjoy your time dear parents this much is true
The God above I know and love
Will surely deal with you!

~

TRUTH

I just know you aren't prepared for what I have to say
I've never told you because I've been afraid
Please sit and make yourself comfortable, Mother
I know that for years you raised us alone after Daddy died
I know you think you loved us with all your heart and soul
Now that I have my own family, I must speak the truth.
Each night, from age seven, when you were at work
My stepdad came into my room and raped me!
At first he'd put me to bed and allow me a piece of candy
That was our little secret between friends.
Then he'd read me bedtime stories curled up next to me
After a while he'd ask for a kiss on the lips—another secret
He'd say, "You are so special to me"
Slowly he'd start to touch me under my nightgown
In the place you said to never show anyone but you
Then one night you had an argument before going to work
That night he didn't make me feel special at all
He pulled my panties off and forced himself inside me

Pieces of me broke then, and I haven't found them yet
I remember when you saw how red I was down there
You put an ointment on me, told me to keep quiet about it.
That I shouldn't tell anyone.

Well? Truth is you knew he raped me
Truth is, you sacrificed your daughter to keep a man around
I paid the price for a few dollars placed in your hand
Truth is, I know you never loved me. I could never know my
Child was being raped and stay with such a monster.
How could you lay beneath a man who laid atop your child?
There is a special place for you in hell, Mother Dear.
So, there you have it—"I've told you the TRUTH."
Truth is, you wanted to know if I knew you were aware
Of what you allowed to be done to me.
Truth is, I've never told anyone. I am one damaged adult among
many. So many adults carry secrets from their messed up child-
hoods. That's why so many people cannot thrive.
Truth is, I sometimes wonder if my husband is a monster too.
You had the nerve to tell your children, "Be the matter what it
may always speak the truth". When you were and still are such
a liar.
Truth is, I hope your place in hell is hotter than anywhere else
there.
Truth is, forgiveness is from God so go ask him for it. I don't
have any for you Mother Dear!
Truth is…sometimes the truth is best left buried.

REGRET

That irritating coulda, woulda, shoulda. I honestly have no regrets. Sometimes I wish I had done certain things earlier, but then I know everything happens in God's time, and His timing is best for me. For all the sickening, aggravating people we meet—they have taught us something, brought us to self-awareness on some level. Or, at the very least, you pray to God that you are never allowed to be like that. Until we die, we will meet people who are agents of the devil and hate that we have the joy of Christ and try to dampen our spirits. But pray for them and rest them right at the foot of the cross. Ask the Lord to deal with them. Go as far as asking him to remove them from your life in one way or the other. He has done it for me several times. Jesus gives me a joy that nobody can understand, and He'll do it for you too. Until you meet somebody here on earth that's willing to die on a cross for your sins and offer you eternal life, nobody should be allowed to steal the joy Christ gives you. So today, decide to have no regrets moving forward. Everything happens for a reason!

REGRETS BENEATH THE RUBBLE

You died in Tower 1 that day
I remember you'd been sick
Physically and of me.
Things were so bad that you'd broke sick leave.
Rushed out the house on the wings of an argument
Didn't even realize you wore two different socks
"I wish you were dead" was the last thing I screamed at you.

Still mad as hell I spoke your name in twisted ways
Grabbing your brand-new shirts, I threw them in a bin and
poured bleach on them, feeling a bit of gladness.
Spent due to anger I fell on the bed, upset that I'd picked
a fight just to avoid telling you I was pregnant. I figured I
wouldn't let you get attached by involving you further.
I planned to abort this little replica of you. In turmoil
I fell asleep.

I dreamt of me falling and you catching me—
the way we used to.
"I'll always love you," you told me while I slept. I awoke to the
sound of screams on TV. Still on my side I ignored it...until I
heard that "Tower 1 was hit by a plane."
Bolt upright I sat, frantically, foolishly searching for your face
in the crowd. I tried calling—nothing. I must still be dreaming.

Roads were blocked. Service was down certain places.
The days that passed were a blur. Your personal effects in-
cluded a pair of mismatched socks and the wedding band
I'd placed on your finger two years prior. We'd always fought
about you not wearing it. Yet, mad as you were, you wore it on
that day. Faithful to the end. I had tarried where fools reside.

Our son is growing well. I tell him all the good things about
you. I told him you weren't even feeling well that day the
towers fell, but that you loved us so very much that you insist-
ed on providing for your family regardless. I tell him what a
wonderful husband you were. Nothing about how foolish I was.
If I could do it all again, I would love you like you loved me. I
would love you WELL!

～

WHEN PEACE RETURNS

In the vast blue sea now colored red
Arms, legs, helmets, dreams of the dead.
If God is on our side, just who is on theirs?
From the first day this war began
I've shed so many tears.

Husbands, many who left home
Earning wives long sleepless nights.
Lonely, frightened mother's sons

Who never got to say goodbye.
War is such an ugly wretch
She breeds just so much sorrow!
Just when will she ever have her fill?
How many more souls must she borrow?

I pray for the day when we'll all be colorblind,
When "Good morning" and a smile from lips
Won't add stress to our minds.

When time will stop at a pleasant place
When all evil thoughts will be erased.
Will I be around when peace returns?
'Til that day shows its face, my starving heart yearns.

∼

THIS FIRE IN MY VEINS

All alone I sit here, invisible.
Needles for the piercing, found next to the dumpster.
Some black vestige still coating the walls of the syringe.
But, it will work…
A strong strip of cloth, someone's old bandana.
My poison from the guy who made me do unspeakable things to him to get it. Nah, he couldn't possibly come from a mother.
He knows how desperate I am, so he used me. But I got the last laugh. He doesn't know I left him with the gift that keeps on giving.

All around me I can hear people going about their lives—invisible. The prick to my skin is sharp. As I press the plunger, the sweet heat that flows through me makes me stop seeing, hearing, worrying. I don't want to be a drug user. I don't want to be this way—claimed by the streets and abused by destiny. But just for a few hours I can forget.

Even in my state of forgetting, I remember:
The night when they came into our little cottage and shot my dad, raped my mom and hung my brother. When the three of them savagely raped the twelve-year-old girl I used to be. They took my innocence, destroyed my mind and removed any possibility of me becoming a mother. Robbing me of my innocence. Forcing me to go through the system that spat me out the first chance it got.
Don't judge me! We are all only one stoplight away from a wreck.

~

THE HOLIDAYS

All through the holiday season, I've watched otherwise sensible people become unhinged. As an EMT, the holidays are a time when folks commit suicide, walk away from home, disappear. We were prepared for the slit wrists, swallowed pills, cars that would "mysteriously" run off the road, alcoholics, etc. Because I answered those calls for so many years I can easily spot, hear or read a "battle." When that reflection hits, that a whole year has passed and nothing happened that they desired, they flip. When they add up the years of "sameness," it turns them into beasts.

But I know a guy. His name is Jesus, who, if you trust Him and serve Him in your heart, His goodness will make every day like Christmas, Valentine's Day, or your birthday. He has the power to break every single yoke of bondage over your life and set you free of all your expectations. Believe it or not, what you expect isn't BIG enough or GOOD enough for him to grant you. What you are waiting on is probably a blessing for someone else. Blessings come in sizes, fashioned for each of us individually. Therefore mine will squeeze the life out of you and yours will kill me slowly!

Call on him. Call on Jesus; allow him to break every chain over your life and walk into this year free of expectation. People love to say, "You expect too much." Truth is, we don't expect enough—if we did, we'd trust him fully. He'll make your head spin. Isn't it wonderful that God knows just what we need? YES! Indeed it is wonderful! I'm praying for you!

NO ONE TOLD ME

No one told me at birth my first cry signaled pain.
My spirit tried to warn me of what it already knew
That life would try to best itself, attempting to kill me
Every step of the way.

No one told me that the womb I was thrust from
Was the safest place I'd ever be.
The heart that I'd heard beating there belonged to Mom
The only one who would ever love me unconditionally

No one told me at three years old I'd see things no three-year-
old should see. I wasn't told that folks love a baby more when
it isn't born yet—not when it keeps you up at night, crying be-
cause it's scared of something.

No one told me as a teen things would start happening to my
body that would make me more visible in an embarrassing way.
Or that "black womanhood" would signal a time when I was
expected to start disappearing, stop speaking, stop thinking for
myself, because it's a man's world.

No one told me that I'd be expected to forfeit my dreams for a
knight in shining armor, who would lock me in a castle away
from the rest of the kingdom—taking his pleasure and leaving
me filled with little princes and princesses who sucked my soul
of all its meat, until the whites of the bones were visible.
No one told me that love had conditions that would never be
mine. That unless I walked a certain way, cooked dinner just

right, or wore the right shade of ruby-red lipstick, my knight would become enraged and beat me mercilessly. That I'd get the chance to watch my skin change from pink red to various shades of puss yellow green, or that the pain would be so overwhelming.

No one told me that menopause would almost drive me insane. That it would come at a time when I'd just come to realize that I had never had the chance to embrace my womanhood, yet I was being stripped of it. No one told me my knight in shiny tinfoil would come to call me old and ugly. That he'd seek his pleasures far and wide from firmer breasts and less wrinkled thighs.

No one told me that life could be so bad that a person could come to dream of a visit from death, or that it could seem more beautiful than life...

Now I lay me down to sleep...

No one told me that I would watch my own funeral. Who the hell are all these people? Why on earth are they crying now, when I had so much they could have cried for while I breathed?

These hypocrites never visited or cared. My knight in wrinkled tinfoil with a cane by his side has the nerve to be crying. No one told me that he'd be consoled by a nurse, one-third his age, with breasts made of plastic barely contained by strained, too-thin cloth. No one told me I'd be tortured until death. I sure wish someone told me.

I SAID GOODBYE TODAY

In a suit of white in your casket you laid
I know God was with me throughout this day
Six months, twelve hours, ten minutes you stayed
For we were happy, we planned and we prayed.

That night you stopped breathing, I felt I did too
Today was a blur, but what can I do...
Here just for a moment to change and repair
Release me from torment—set me free from fear

See I never knew a mother I'd be
You gave me those eyes, just so I could see
That mothers are made, not born day to day
For this I say thank you, you showed me the way

The faces were blurred, the church packed so tight
Condolences much like fast fading light
The hymns sang to comfort they did no such thing
This pain I feel is too deep within

Dear Lord I pray as I sit here tonight
For every pained mother whose child lost the fight

Be they near or far touch their hearts, show them love
This healing we need only comes from above.

GOD KNOWS OUR HEARTS

Remember, the position of our hearts and minds are the only things that can keep us out of heaven. Too many nice things and loved ones will be there for me not to go. You see the evidence, how much God's promises are coming to fruition one after the other. I do not desire to get dressed on Sunday and hoot and holler in church to make an impression, because none of the impressed can get me into the gates. What I desire is genuine purity of heart and a deep relationship with Christ. I want to see my mama again, and I'd like to be able to say to folks there, "That guy used to be my earthly husband, and he's still fine." God knows our hearts.

THE WISHING WELL

At the old wishing well I sat
While pondering life's pathway
Looking at her peacefulness
Why couldn't life be just that way?
I besought the gods of hope
As my first dime I threw
To banish every thought of war
A safer earth for me and you
I bartered with another dime
As her waters rippled and changed
A splash of hers jumped and kissed my cheek
As cruelty was rearranged
I came across a penny next
As shiny as can be
On this I placed a simple wish
Minds in bondage would all be set free
A quarter was next to touch my palm
On that bright sunny day
I wished on all the scrolls of old
That poverty be taken away
I tossed a brand new nickel next

As a couple flicked a dime
'Twas then I asked the gods of love
To leave all their troubles behind
If a few coins could change the world

It would have happened a long time ago
And why things change yet stay the same?
I guess we may never know...

❦

ANGELS

Blessed angels' wings spread wide
All around me, by my side
Assigned to me each with pure love
Protection sent straight from above

I'll never know the things you see
The awful things you've kept from me
Yet, here I stand because of you
Blessed to have another view

Sometimes I fret because I'm late
Unknowingly I've cheated fate
Ten minutes earlier, five minutes more
Would mean I'd stand before death's door

Aware of you, thankful I am
To have you angels in God's plan
I feel so loved, I feel no fear
To know that you are standing near.

GOD'S GRACE IS SUFFICIENT

God's grace is sufficient. Not our kind of sufficiency either. We give the "just enough" kind, the "put on your glasses to see it" kind. But HALLELUJAH, God's grace is limitless! Honestly, when a woman is loved by God, how will she allow herself to be courted by fools here on earth?

CAUGHT UP!

I was sitting on a park bench having lunch when it happened. Suddenly the air took on a disposition that I've never felt before. The couple up ahead started running; soon the man was airborne...

But his form changed, he became a bright light.

On the main road accidents started, the taxi ran into a tree.

The bus stopped moving and the driver started cursing at the car in front of him, but there was no one to hear as it was empty. Suddenly a woman started screaming a few benches over.

Her baby carriage was now empty

People ran, cried, rejoiced, screamed

Then an elderly couple holding hands looked at each other and smiled as they took flight. Two bright lights intertwined, a Hallelujah that sounded like a giggle coming from them.

Suddenly I understood. THIS IS THE RAPTURE!

Was I ready? I began to question myself as the earth rumbled around me. I wondered if I too would be caught up.

I had always heard that Christ shall come in the twinkling of an eye.

I wondered would I be among those left behind.

I'd given my life to Christ years ago, but life took over.

Sometimes, I forgot I was saved.

Sometimes, I neglected God.

But He'd always kept me...

Frantic, I realized my last bite of hot dog had turned to mush in my mouth, and I was suddenly cold.

"Will you welcome me, Lord?" I prayed.

I felt cradled as I was lifted.

I felt light, unburdened.

I closed my eyes, getting excited, I couldn't wait to see God's face.

All around me I could hear the most beautiful sound of angels singing.

"The Eastern Gate" was the song they sang....

Caught up..."Hallelujah, I was caught up"

All around me were the other faithful souls.

"Well done, my good and faithful servant."

Wonderful. Counselor. His face is beautiful.

Behind him I see my parents waving at me.

I run to their open arms of light.

Crying, I can't wait to talk to them.

Then a phone rings. There are phones in heaven?
It was only a dream. My phone on the nightstand is ringing.
I let it go to voicemail.
But as I look at my window, a bright light shines through.
A dream. A reminder to be always ready.
What a day…glorious day…that will be.

~

THE MASTER'S PLAN

As I walk through the valley of death
This fear I feel now I will never forget
At the end of the tunnel there's such a bright light
Encouraging much eternal fight

Sometimes my feet feel oh so sore
Most times my back can't bend anymore
Salty tears spill out of my eyes
There are so many shades of gray in the skies

I bend my head and start to pray
I ask the Master to lead the way
Then suddenly my steps get light
All of the wrong things are made right
I place my hands in those of love
As guidance and strength I'm fed from above

I realize I'm no longer alone
Of this I'm sure down in my bones

A sweet breeze dries up all my tears
A cushion softens all my fears
My back is suddenly very straight
As through my veins course endless faith

Oh! My Lord I almost fell
But as the light grew brighter, I started to yell
At the end of this long tunnel I finally am
I look back to where my journey began

It seemed like it would never end
Sometimes I wished I had a friend
But, had I just opened up my eyes
Looked past those gray clouds in the skies
I would have seen the Master's hands
And in his palms my unique plan.

≈

DYING EMPTY

When the time comes around and my journey is done
Perhaps, just perhaps every victory won't be won
But gladly I'll go resting my weary head
With Jesus I'm sure just this flesh will be dead

We are put here to love and to teach...to care
A life filled with Christ is a life with no fear
To give all we can. We are blessed just to bless
To be there for each other as we go through life's tests

Until then I will be here, your duty to fulfill
Patiently doing as is your will
Strength you will give for each daily fight
I serve a God of power, glory and might

You've gone to prepare my heavenly home
Of this I am sure, as this troubled earth I roam
'Til then I'll be patient your love I will share
Encouraging others "For Jesus, prepare"

When it's time blessed Lord, willing, empty I'll come
Perhaps, just perhaps every victory won't be won
Tired and weary yet happy I'll be
Because finally your wondrous face I shall see.

TENDER MOMENTS

Tender moments soft as clouds
Seldom do they come around
With velvet threads they touch our souls
Their memories warm through winter's cold
These moments like a camera
Form pictures in our minds.
The tender softness of them,
Leave all bad thoughts behind.
These are the times I treasure
As your warmth courses through my soul.
This warmth it binds and keeps me
With a strength that never grows old!
So treasured are these few moments,
Bound in my heart by lock and key,
By far they're much more precious
Than any gift ever purchased for me.

≈

THE LORD LOVES US

First you gave me the right parents, who gave me a chance to see God in the midst of a couple, and the way true love strengthens you. Then you took me far away into a place that would lay the groundwork for my life. A hard, strange place that would put me to work but give me benefits and an education that would last me a lifetime. Health, strength, and guidance have always been given to me in full measure. You've allowed me to see so many places on this globe, experience so much, because you know I like to travel by sea or air. Opportunity, opportunity, opportunity! I'm still amazed at the way you point me in their direction, still amazed at the way you uproot and remove, still amazed that you remember that prayer I prayed as a young girl, that you remove what no longer serves me from my life. You promised that I would be honored if I honor you and I'm living it. Then you told me plain as day:

[1]Now the LORD had said unto Abram, Get thee out of thy country, and from thy kindred, and from thy father's house, unto a land that I will shew thee:

[2]And I will make of thee a great nation, and I will bless thee, and make thy name great; and thou shalt be a blessing:

[3]And I will bless them that bless thee, and curse him that curseth thee: and in thee shall all families of the earth be blessed (Genesis 12:1-3).

That took a lot! But I'm sure glad I listened, because to watch you work is amazing! So today I come boldly before the throne with a grateful spirit to say, "Thank you, Lord." Thank you for the perfect alignment of people, places and things. Thank you for giving me lush harvest, blessings without sweat. Thank you for giving me exceedingly and abundantly above all that I could ever ask or imagine. Continue to guide, guard and protect me, Lord. I know you gave me the power to open my mouth and command my needs to be met, so I will continue to do that with no fear, as you did not give us a spirit of fear. Thank you for my husband, because the power of TWO is greater than one, every day of the week. Thank you for loving me Lord. I love you too. I'm thankful that I am your special girl.

LOVE

LOVE does not hurt

LOVE is not confusing

LOVE walks in certainty

LOVE does not care what you think of it

LOVE is confident

LOVE protects, provides, teaches

LOVE restores

LOVE makes plans for your future

LOVE is proud of you

LOVE speaks kindly of you behind your back

LOVE can't see you suffer and not assist you

LOVE is coming if you are in trouble

LOVE gives you one of the two it has, or ALL, and stays without for the time being, if that is necessary

LOVE is kind

LOVE is the greatest force there is

LOVE makes you sleep well at night

LOVE is secure

LOVE is beautiful

LOVE gives without asking

LOVE studies you in order to please you

LOVE allows a woman to feel like one

LOVE makes a man do what he should do

LOVE builds you up

LOVE adds to your life and replaces what is lost

LOVE enhances better to make it best

LOVE shows on you

LOVE is everything.

≈

AT A LOSS FOR WORDS

I can't believe words fail me
They have the nerve to avoid me
I've been careful with you, developed trust
Help me, I beg you. Help me, you must!

Afraid I lay in this cold room
Eyes fixed on me, I feel nothing but gloom.
Questions thrown yet no words to speak.
If you don't help me the outcome will be bleak.

Sweating palms and shaking knees
I beg of you to help me, please.
An aging fool I'm thought to be
I know I'm not, now help them see…

When words are tossed, words should return.
The backs of my eyes are beginning to burn.
You've betrayed me, a once thought loyal friend.
I thought you'd stay with me to the end.

Even my memory is faint this day.
Words that were used, even they won't play.
I just can't remember what I once knew.
If ever words fail you, what will you do?

Old and frail my thoughts wiped clean.
Why do they stare, why are they being so mean?
I know that I know what I have to say.
But if I'm blessed with tomorrow, I'll forget today.

I hate Alzheimer's!

≈

WHAT FLOWERS MEAN TO ME

When I'm old and gray and
My eyes grow dim
What good will flowers do me then?
When memory fades
When I am lost to where or when
What good will flowers do me then?

When cast aside
An aging hen
What good will flowers do me then?

When perfumed petals
Are not my friends
What good will flowers do me then?

They'll flood my casket
Beginning to end
But, what good will flowers do me then?

Bring them now
While I can see
I'll tell you what flowers mean to me.

～

WILL YOU CARE FOR ME?

Will you care for me when I grow old
When my sight is not so very bold
When dark confusion clouds my mind
Will you, my love, cease to be kind?
When my steps are frail and weak
When my lips forget to speak
When my ears forget to hear
Will you then forget to care?

43

Once a man and twice a child
We will all leave strength behind
Don't forget we all must be
Aware of this shared destiny

But even though my skin may show
A wrinkled map. Where did I go?
My heart will still beat for you, you see?
I ask you now, "Will you care for me?"

~

A WOMAN'S MIND

A woman's mind is her own library
Some memories bound with leather pure
Stacked wall to wall, with books from floor to ceiling
There is only one key to that old door

So complex are these countless collections
Some old, some new, all stored with perfect care
She doesn't loan some of these very special treasures
There are so many private specials there
Behind one case there is a safe so grand and shiny
With memories, wishes, dreams too great to tell
It also holds things just too awful for discussion
That she may mention if you get to know her well

There is a chair there that she finds very relaxing
Where she sits when life is just too much to bear
Soft music plays there on an old radio beside her
It's the place she goes to where she feels no fear

In her library are memories long forgotten
With dusty covers, bookmarked tassels bare

She runs her fingers gently o'er them just to stir them
Every second of her life kept safely there

If you should see her lost in thought please be quiet
Respect the moment that is hers and so divine
You are so blessed you are allowed to witness
Her relaxed within the library of her mind

∾

MY GIRDLE TRIED TO KILL ME!

Leave that girdle over there; let it strangle its own self. My God! Our pulse races as we stare death in the face trying our best to navigate one leg of this murderer at a time. Of course, now would be the time we have to pee. So we do the lopsided shuffle to the throne, almost killing ourselves as we plop unevenly down, thinking it's the last time we fall backwards, imagining our head connecting with the porcelain, and company finding us in a state that rivals a car up on a hoist. Looking like a pretzel and feeling the same, we somehow manage to wipe the falling tears of our laughing lady parts.

A foolish idea that seemed bright at the time: We think we should try to pull our undies, hose and girdle up at once, one side at a time. We steel our thoughts against this wave of impossibility that is sure to hit and we heave all three garments up left side first forcefully. Fresh hell! A finger is now stuck somewhere between these arguing garments in an extremely unnatural position, and once you figure out that you should fight for its independence, you tug. Something happens. You are now wedged halfway between the commode and the incredibly small space that serves no purpose. Some part of your butt cheek is wedged against the seat of the commode, which has decided to play doctor by poking you in ways that should offer a glass of wine first.

Your heart beats furiously, sweat pours off you, while positioned like an anteater, you feel a cool breeze in places you didn't know existed. Fear propels your bowels to become active and you will drown in its issue if you do not right yourself back into a seated position. Summoning the strength of ten fit men, you manage to hoist yourself on the seat, just as your innards scream loud enough to remind you who is boss. Finally you have made up your mind to end this foolishness and cut to shreds any form of restrictive garment you own…as soon as you get up.

What sorcery is this? There is no more toilet paper next to you. You swear it was there a minute ago when you used it last. Of course it is across from you in the storage cabinet that you can see, bulging at the hinge for all the ill-arranged rolls of paper inside it. So you say a prayer, calm your nerves, and feel your pulse slow down almost to normalcy.

Let's assess this situation. You are half naked, halfway strangled by your garments. You need to wipe yourself, it smells bad, and on top of it all, you need another shower for all the sweating you have done, and you are sure you've been in there hours and you must be late. Your friend is going to kill you! You have decided to swallow pride and do the poop shuffle across to the cabinet. You attempt to stand, and you shuffle twice—just twice—then you fall…HARD! On the tile. I think it is fair to say that these garments are staging a revolt and have made their mind up to play nasty and trip you.

The phone rings while you are lying there in pain, dragging your body to the cabinet. My God, it's your friend calling to say she had made a mistake and the function that you had almost killed yourself getting ready for was in fact being held tomorrow. Laughing hysterically you swear to yourself, dirty butt and all, "I shall burn every girdle I own, let my parts fall where they may, they are mine, damn it, they are mine!"

~

LET THAT LI'L WOMAN SPEAK!

Don't you "shush" her, let her talk
Her voice needs to be heard!
Stop telling her to sit still all the time
Never let her wild spirit die
She will need that bit of wildness to survive
When those bad grades come later
Ask her what's wrong... children go through, too
Stop calling her "fat," you'll make her self-conscious
You are the parent!
Instead, be careful what you feed her
Tell her she's beautiful every chance you get
That way she'll know already when that thirsty boy says it
Tell her she is worthy because she was born

The fact that she was—is—enough!
Balance correction with accolades
A healthy emotional state invites communication
When the troubles come in school, she'll trust you
She will run to the safe place of home for solutions
Don't you mess that li'l woman up!
She has a right to walk in her confidence
Help to build her, give her the shoes of greatness
Keep changing their size as the need for bigger ones arise

When she wonders if she can, tell her "Yes, baby, you can."
Love her little fears away
Be her example
The wind in her sails
When the world comes at her
She will not forget her foundation.

$\sim$

FORBIDDEN FRUIT

Meet me in my dreams again
Where there is much ado about something.
Where I can sit in your shade and taste the juicy fruit of you,
sticky-sweet on my fingers, running down my chin until I've
had my fill.

Where closed eyes mean I'm awake, and we are but invisible, unrestrained, untamed, hungry and unbothered. Firm fruit in my palm, ripe and ready to eat. Such an amazing symphony of discord. The smell of this fruit so heady that while I eat I wonder when will my next taste be…

Forbidden fruit we are, in baskets belonging to others. Dark spots against our souls, where we've sat too long. Ripe—over-ripe! The pungent aroma of our too sweet fruit evident to any sensitive nose. Yet we remain untouched, waiting in vain to be picked up, washed and eaten…

Here though, in my dreams, the bruising of you is welcomed. Each bruised, meaty piece of flesh is licked and kissed—each drop of juice swallowed. Spectacular flavors slowly flowing down my throat. Each bite more delicious than the last. Several layers of taste delighting and surprising my senses.

How can one piece of fruit be so pleasing?

Finally—the seed. What I've been working towards. Give it up. Wedged in cords holding it tightly in place. I rock it, I roll it…dangerously firm it is. Finally a pop. I am left with a sticky face and hands…until next time you meet me in my dreams again…

~

I REMEMBER WHEN…

You made love to me where the water meets the shore. We lay there breathing for each other. My out, your in, and back again, not knowing the end or the beginning. Each kiss tattooed my spirit in a way that the ink still remains fresh, even today. The smell of your skin against mine, like something to be bottled, heady, sensual, DEEP. You have the ability to bring to life my sleeping soul. Oh! Drunk I was with you as the waves crashed against the shore, coaxing us to mimic its rhythm. Under your skilled hands I am able to reach the very edge of ecstasy. When I break into bits and pieces you take the time to gather them all, putting me back together—more complete than before. In our joining you manage to fill my veins, cells, marrow with you, in a way that only you can. The salty taste of the water against your brow quenches my thirst yet leaves me thirsty. Crazed sanity was what you gave to me that night. You never missed one part of me as you loved me, taking your time—over and over. My love, why did it have to end? I still remember when…

WATER DANCE

I am jealous of the way that water sprays against your skin.
The way that washcloth touches places I never will.
That warm water washes away secrets I'll never know down the
drain—to God knows where.
Sweet soap kisses your dark, pretty flesh in ways that make me
grind my teeth.
Steam romances you, teases your thoughts as it glances at you.
Allowed in your space. It even fogs up the mirrors trying to get a
glimpse of you.
I hear you humming…
Such pleasure is yours…
What could you have done to scrub your flesh so ferociously?
What memories do you try to wash away?
Lost in thoughts of you I missed the silence—the water has
stopped.
Still humming from your water dance, you emerge.
Huge smile on your handsome face, you have the nerve to tell
me how good it was.
Towel wrapped around your strong waist.
Broad chest, muscles rippling as you walk towards me
Evidence of this water dance all over you…wet, glistening.
I remove your towel, kneel on the bed.
I offer my tongue to your shoulder
Come…let me help you dry.
What water has left for me is immaculate.

❧

UNDEFILED (For W. G. ❤)

Come to me sweet husband
I've planned to lay you over there
I have prepared for you a table
No enemies are present—just US.
All day I've missed you
Let me help you out those clothes
Draw you a bath—
Wash the world off you—
Tell me all about your day
Umm, your shoulders are tense
Relax under my loving hands
Oh, you want to wash my hair?
Scrub my back?
Go right ahead
Do what you want to me
I want you to kill me and bring me back to life tonight
These petals scent the room so nicely
This music is so tender
The towel that dries us like the strings of a guitar
Between us glides making hot spots even hotter
Really—why dry just to get wet again?

Let me oil your bald head
Feel those muscles ripple beneath your gorgeous flesh
The darker the berry they say

Yes…I wanna get to that sweet juice
Come husband dear, just lay right here for me
This meeting is licensed, blessed and approved
We can do everything and then some
Our marriage bed is UNDEFILED!

MY PERSONAL TESTIMONY

Two reasons why I'm THANKFUL! (Just two out of countless.) In November 2003, I was at work in the early hours of the morning in the passenger seat of the ambulance, when a drunk driver (F-250) overtook several cars and banged into my side of the rig. He pushed us over the side of a hill, and we came to a stop just shy of a sugar mill, in the area of Anna's Hope on St. Croix. While driving during the day, you can peek through the bushes and look down to see the horse that's usually tied there. By some miracle, the horse was not there, and we didn't hit the mill. The door came in on me, the windshield shattered, and I banged my head somewhere; I still have the scar. They cut the pieces of the ambulance from around me to get to me. I remember thinking, "Lord, don't you dare let these people have to call my parents to upset them with any foolishness this morning." My co-worker, Mr. Anthony, wormed his way into that mess and put his hand on me. He said, "I'm going to get you out." Then he made himself ten times smaller, put a collar on me and lifted me on the backboard.

My boss sat in the back of the unit with me. My coordinator stayed with me in the hospital. She morphed into a mother and looked about me. The month I was out from work took me home to recuperate. Every day, my husband—he was just a friend at the time—would spend time with me at my parents' house. A few days after the accident, I spoke to him by phone and he said, "I want you to come home—do you have the money? Do you need me to come travel with you?" Mom and Dad would come upstairs to help me bathe. Dad insisted I walk down the stairs to come to eat, so that I would have to walk back up them. The relationship flourished between my husband and I. So I am thankful for life and all the good that came from that accident.

There was a picture of the ambulance on the front page of the newspaper the day after. The story read, "Two EMTs pulled from wreckage, shocked that they are alive." But MY GOD IS AWESOME! He was not ready to take me yet!

Then Thanksgiving 2011, my husband and I were here in Florida—Ft. Lauderdale to be exact. While everywhere was closed, we went to Dunkin' Donuts for breakfast because there was nowhere else open. I remember apologizing to him for not being able to prepare a meal for him. We had just left from the doctor's the day before, where I got some awful news. News that again miraculously turned around for good. We filled our bellies, got to the airport and made our way back. See, what the enemy fashions to destroy you is most times a blessing in disguise. For all the bad stuff, Winston Gore has been there to witness it. That's not a mistake. It's all in the master plan. So when you see me praising God and giving him thanks, just know that the bits and pieces of my life have made me very thankful. I am blessed and highly favored! This is why I will give my last to somebody. I'm just happy to be alive to give it. This is why I love—live—work so passionately. Everyday I give thanks, but around Thanksgiving each year, I reflect on the holidays past that could have been my last. God's guidance, love and tender mercies to you all.

Isaiah 55:11 MSG

Just as the rain and snow descend from the skies and don't go back until they've watered the earth…making things grow and blossom…So will the words that come out my mouth not come back empty-handed. They'll do the work I sent them to do.

THE EMT'S PRAYER

"Thank you, Dear Lord" is the first thing we say
For breath to start another day
As we race along these streets of need
Please go before us, we beg you to lead
Open up our humble minds
As help to give, we seek to find
We ask that we'll compassionate be
To someone whose loved one may today be set free
There are times when a patient just needs a friend
We ask in these moments your patience to lend
Dear Father, through us, please speak those words
The ones for which the troubled heart yearns
In those moments when the end draws near
Please take away our patients' fear
Unwavering strength we ask of you
As we do this work we love to do
Please give our hands a loving touch
Without words it can say so much
However heavy the coat my partner wears
I pray dear Lord its weight you'll bear
Protect our families one and all
Place around them a protective wall

As we, earth's angels commissioned by you
Give our best as you'd have us do
We ask that all the lives we touch this day
Will benefit from having us pass their way.

AMEN.

MY MAGIC PEN

I was six years old and playing outside
To tell you the truth I was trying to hide
Behind the house, next to a tree
The coolest thing awaited me

There in the dirt just peeking out
Was a blue pen. Shocked I opened my mouth
Shiny, unscarred by the dirt
I'd soon find out this treasure's worth

I touched the pen; it shocked my hand
I'd have to figure out a plan
At six this find was such a dream
The most beautiful thing I'd ever seen

Upon my bed I sat to write
This feeling impossible to fight
It made me want to write some things
Giving my thoughts flight on wings

The ink within it never dries
Writing still makes me high as the sky
I always will remember when
I was blessed with my magic pen

❧

"A WAY WITH WORDS"

"You have such a way with words." "Not really," is usually my reply. I seldom say "Thank you." Truth is, WORDS are little terrors that have loud parties inside your head at all hours. They hold your thoughts hostage and refuse to free them unless they are allowed to "Be themselves," jumping from your lips naked, at the wrong time, in the weirdest situations.

WORDS are vagabonds—murderous heathens who assault you on the way to the toilet at three in the morning and hold your eyelids open until they have their way—let out to play across the computer screen or on an unsuspecting notepad.

WORDS haunt you at times when there is no way to get them out: no pen, no paper, no screen. Suddenly you hear them laughing hysterically in your head—calling you a fool.

So I don't have a way with WORDS. WORDS have their way with me...and I enjoy it!

CREATIVE MIND

Creative mind
Impossible to contain
Like water you take the shape of anything
Adaptable to situation
Dressed words for any occasion
Creative mind

MY SON: A Letter From A Young Mother

My Dear Son K,

In a strange land, far away from home, I gave birth to you. I was nineteen. I was alone, scared, unsure. I had been told things: "Your life is over." "No man will ever marry you." "You'll never amount to anything," and much more of which I'll spare you. I'd had protected sex, but there is no protection against what God permits. Sometimes we must go through storms to appreciate calm. My landlady, may she be blessed—old, southern, Caucasian lady, would send her husband down to my cabin with a meal daily for me. As a mother herself, she had taken me under her wings. Seen me for the lost child I was. The day before I labored with you, I remember telling her how painful my back was. She told me, "You're almost ready, chile." Then she prayed over me. I am aware of every angel that was put in place for me throughout my life. You should be aware of your angels as well. She prayed safety for my journey, promised to bring back some stewed okras, they eased labor she said—then she was gone.

Seventeen hours of labor followed.

In a cold, "almost-ready labor room," surrounded by other couples and their family; those contractions came at me like the devil comes from hell. A nineteen-year-old child pushed a baby from the safest place he'll ever be. Four pounds, six and a half ounces of what will always be my greatest blessing. We had made it. You were alive. I loved you before I knew you. I thanked the Lord.

Then came reality.

You were born with asthma. I was a service member, so our care was wonderful. I was given a large bag of medications to leave the hospital with. I looked at that bag, compared it to your little frame and decided I wasn't going to give you that mess. In that little cabin on the lake I held your little body and I said, "Lord, we sit here alone, far away from all that makes sense. They are telling me my child is sick, and I don't believe them. What I do believe in is your healing power, and I ask that you visit it on us going forward. Touch this little soul you've allowed me to care for, from the crown of his head to the soles of his feet. Right now I give his life back to you and ask that it be lived for your honor and glory. Let my child thrive Lord. Amen! I put you down on that old couch. I picked that bag of medicine up and threw them in the garbage. Well, my prayer was answered. At twenty-four, you are healthy and shall continue to be.

Motherhood will grow you up quickly. I found myself having to make choices that were extremely hard at times. A simple thing like the next meal would be missed, so you could eat. But I was always a woman who believed in the power of prayer, so I never forgot who I was. I trusted God. I knew that every road we walk is for a reason, and I'm always curious to know what is on the other end of each. I knew even then that God promised to do exceedingly, abundantly above all that we could ever ask for or think. I believed!

I wish I could reach every young mother out there who is scared and confused. The young ladies who have been convinced that they don't deserve love because somebody told them they are trash for bringing new life into this world, that JOY comes in the morning. I wish I could tell them to hold on. I wish I could tell them that God allowed that seed in their belly, and that come what may He'll keep them. I wish I could tell them to avoid that abortion clinic they are encouraged to go to, to even save the money they are given to have that abortion. I wish I could tell them to ignore all those voices around them that push them to give up. I wish I could tell them all that if I could make it, so will they. I want them to know that I am praying for them wherever they may be, and that they are not alone.

It takes a village.

Your grandparents love me so much, that they loved you too. If it weren't for them I don't know what would have happened to me or you. Son, I love you with all my heart. I want you to know I am proud of the man you've become. I want you to know that you were born for such a time as this, and I am still humbled to this day that I was the chosen vessel to bring you here. I am ever striving to make you continually proud of me. Those things that you struggle with today will be a faint memory tomorrow. So it makes no sense to ever sell your soul. Remember the ones you expect answers from, get their answers from God, so cutting out the middle man gets the job done quicker.

You've made it, son, my one and only. I pray continued blessings on you and on the future seeds from your loins and nothing but goodness and tender mercies over your life. May your cup be so full on this leg of your journey that it overflows on all who are to come. Never forget He who keeps you. You are my inspiration.

I love you dearly
Your Praying Mother,
Renna

~

PHOENIX

phoe·nix

/fēniks/

noun

(in classical mythology) a unique bird that lived for five or six centuries in the Arabian desert, after this time burning itself on a funeral pyre and rising from the ashes with renewed youth to live through another cycle; a person or thing regarded as uniquely remarkable in some respect.

I will rise again
Much stronger next time around
The last six hundred years I got it wrong
I've made mistakes that I must right
Sometimes I flew too low not trusting myself enough
At other times too high; false confidence
There were many attempts to clip my wings
Too many attempts to cage me
I've been shot down, stoned and hurt
The masses have tried to destroy me
It bothers many that I've been allowed to live so long
Never has it crossed their minds just what it takes to fly
The strength required to stay up here each day
Or how much wisdom is needed to stay alive

Sometimes it's hard to even hunt for food
Never do they consider that the winds are harsh
That they come against me sometimes with such force

I hunt to survive, but they hunt to end my survival
I am tired! My time of flight is over for now
I can hear the call of the gods sent with the last wind
With direction of the pyre; time when it is hottest
Not too high, not too low, but just right I fly this time
I feel no fear. I will awaken with strength next rising
Next time all will be right.
Into the fire I go
Don't cry for me
For I will rise again

STANDARDS

Remember, your standards should be higher than your heels, your spirit should be sweeter than your choice of perfume for the day, and there should be more money inside your purse than on your arm; remember you determine your worth, not your spouse or the man or woman of the minute. Not everyone will like you, but that's okay—if we were all alike the news would never be worth watching. It truly takes all kinds. Good manners will take you places. Rudeness and filthy behavior takes you nowhere fast. Be grateful for *life*, as many are fighting for it at this very moment. Never think anything is too good for you. At the same time, be aware of what just isn't good enough. Once in a while, love on yourself. It is with this practice that you will grow accustomed to loving others. Pray for those who hurt you, as most times it's their own failure and bitterness that leads them to act the fool. Hurt people hurt people. Challenge yourself to do what makes you uncomfortable, to step out of your comfort zone. There is no growth in complacency. Know that God is watching over you. Know that your steps are ordered. Know there are wonders and favor ahead of you if you believe in God and live for him.

SLEEP IS OVERRATED

While you sleep this world is wide awake!
Are you done yet?
Maybe you have arrived!
Only the comfortable rest!

Warm beds and fluffy pillows are for the accomplished
Sweet dreams are just for those with peace of mind
Safety is only for the foolish
Satisfaction for the lazy and the blind

But hungry people never ever turn off
That switch so many people call a brain
They constantly are tuning and refining
The things they know will later cause them pain

They go on and on, there's no time to get weary
An empty basket always will remain
To add those eggs, they wisely must be scattered
They know nothing ventured, nothing gained

They'll splash some water, yawn and keep it moving
Determined to achieve those goals they've set
Misunderstood and laughed at, there are many
Who know nothing's been done by the sleeping yet!

HOLD ON TO YOUR YOU!

Don't let him touch you if you don't feel loved
Many have it backwards, they think the touch brings love
Not so at all. Only those who treasure YOU should be let in
To do otherwise is akin to letting thieves walk through your
home while you smile and nod as they walk by.
You know good and well they come to harm and destroy,
But just to have someone, anyone walk through, we let them...
Bad idea. When you are not loved, no care is taken to remove
Shoes before walking through. So much "mud" is brought into
your life. The stench from the last place he's been comes with
him and stinks up your place. Tell him YOU aren't that thirsty.
Tell him it's been long, but you still remember what that feels
like when a man loves you, and "this ain't it." Tell him love was
so good the last time that it was more than enough to last until
the next time. Ask him if you look like a new, shiny toy. Ask if
your wrapper entices him as he thinks of the crinkly sounds it
will make as it comes off. Oh! He had the nerve to get mad at
YOU for keeping YOU to yourself? Listen, he'll be all right.
Folks grow to hate the people they can't control. That's not your
problem—it's his. You gotta have love to make love. Otherwise
you just need a shower after, your heart is trying to jump out
your chest because even it wonders if you have lost your mind.
Until a man loves and respects you, keep loving and respecting
yourself. Lonely you say? Girl, go get yourself a dog and contin-
ue to *hold on to your you.*

PASS IT ON!

Do not block your blessings! I'm like this: if I have any bit of knowledge, I pass it on. Some people are stingy even with knowledge; they fear you will know more than they do. I, on the other hand, want you to surpass me, and when you are complimented and asked who taught you, and you speak my name—that adds to my bank of BLESSINGS. Everywhere I go I'm told, "You have such a beautiful spirit." When people say that to me, I reply, "That's Christ in me." So I know I'm doing something right. I just ask the Lord to continue to guide me, keep me, continue to go before me, continue to open those doors for me, and supply the right people to hand me the keys. Lord, I feel so blessed! So humbled and amazed. Thank you Jesus. I love you, Lord! The rest of my life is yours.

TOO SHY TO TRY...

"What if they don't like it?"
"But what if they do?"
Make your mind up and do it
Push all the way through

"But what if I fail? I've never done anything right!"
"My life has always been a very huge fight."
Tell you what, my friend, you'll never know.
We first must be born in order to grow

"They said I was a fool."
"Dad said I was a waste."
You were created for a purpose
Your dad does not decide your fate

"But I've been to prison."
"Nobody trusts me anymore."
Belief in your self is all you need in this life
Go ahead, I'll hold your hand, let's walk through that door

∾

BEHIND THESE BARS

I told them I didn't do it
I told them I was never there
As much as I said it
Nobody cared

Twenty years I have withered, wasted my life
Wishing for freedom, a small glimpse of hope
Missed Mom's funeral, Dad's in a home
They said I killed somebody over some dope

I know I look scary—I stand six foot three
Black as deep night, I weigh two-eighty-two
Size fifteen shoes, big britches too
But I've never hurt a fly, that's the truth from me to you

This morning I heard they are setting me free
Something about DNA and evidence I don't really understand
Truth is I'm scared, I have no one out there
They stole my life from me. I was dealt a bad hand

I'm not too smart, school just wasn't for me
Things were hard to remember early on you see

Who will hire a jailbird? A dumb one at that
Apparently I pose a threat even to me

The real thugs and murderers wear suits and high heels
They live somewhere fancy and go to work every day
At the top they give orders, they are never found out
They go to church on Sunday, people ask them to pray

While the innocent poor are arrested and tried
All over the news to distract while they slide
It's bad enough being black—now add trying to hide
I'll let you know how that works, when I'm back on the outside.

BEING TAUGHT THROUGH OTHERS

(Actual names used here)

All this week the Lord has been using people to teach me things. I've always caught on fast. Earlier he showed me Harrison Okene, twenty-nine years old, a cook on a vessel out to sea, lone survivor of twelve. He lived for three days in an air pocket, praying to God to deliver him while he inhaled the rotting stench of the other eleven co-workers and listened to the fish feast on their bodies. Three days he lingered in that vessel. God said to me, "He is like Jonah." Sent me back to study that portion of my Bible. Many days I was literally at sea, on a naval vessel, but I came back. From that I was reminded that God is with me anywhere, in any situation and that gave me comfort.

Then another story flashed on my feed. The story of Alice Herz-Sommer—she's 109. This lady is the oldest-living pianist. She's also a Holocaust survivor. As a young woman in those camps she used the beauty and power of music, compositions from Brahms, Tchaikovsky and others from memory—she played them in that awful place, with death all around her, from memory—this amazed me as she was so stressed at the time. Imagine playing at a concert in hell, while you waited for your number to be called. Little did she know her purpose was to ease the minds of the dying around her. Little did she know her usefulness would sustain her through it. Then came God's deliverance. Music helps to keep us alive.

Then yesterday Nelson Mandela passed, ninety-five years old. Since I became aware of his presence on this globe at a young age, I've always been curious. I'm not in the lot of people who get impressed easily, so I remember my dad explaining to me what his fight was about. I was impressed. I remember his release. I remember Daddy saying to me that many times in life, I will be an army of one. He said not to waver. Even if it's just me, I should stand strong and that in the end God will vindicate me, as nobody else can do. There are three people I really admire in this world. Three that I wish to speak to, sit a spell with, suck up their essence by being in the same room with them. Mr. Mandela is one of them. "Madiba." Regular people let the word *greatness* flow through their mouth like they know what they are saying. But there is a class of individuals on this earth who embody greatness—it's already decided and it's not by our standards. May he rest in the peace he so valiantly fought for. Those twenty-seven years in prison only made him stronger. We'll sit and talk later. We still need to talk.

"The meek shall inherit the earth" (Matthew 5:5). Those three people were used to show me that God can use the least among us to do the greatest. He can make us test our testimony. He can deliver us from ANYTHING. He has promised me many blessings, and I am living them daily. I tell people all the time that when you are living a life for God, it is evident by the fruit you bear. Christian people should live the best life—it is written! So if you find that your soil does not bring you rich harvest, re-examine yourself. Don't look up the road at me, look within. Allow yourself to be used by him—you will see miracles, signs and wonders! Glory be to God.

NEW STATE OF MIND

No more time to waste with you
I've got somewhere to go
Things are green and growing there
Just want you to know

No more time for lollygagging
I've got a time to meet
In this world that's ever changing
We must stay on our feet

I may have to leave you
My journey ahead is long
Unless you get it together
You'll be singing a lonely song

See I'm tired of just talking every day
A change for the better, doing things my way
I must leave you behind, my friend called "Doubt"
These blessings to come—I shall speak from my mouth

≈

GREEN GRASS REQUIRES CONSTANT ATTENTION

Your neighbor's grass is green and beautiful because they invest time and money into taking care of it. Their sprinklers are set to come on at a certain time. They don't allow anyone to walk all over it, and when they get done cutting it, they will even get down and clip the strays with a pair of scissors if they have to. Time, money, love, work!

The time you take to stand behind your curtains hating on that neighbor because of their lawn, you could be tending yours. You can also walk over and say, "Neighbor, your lawn is beautiful. I have always admired it; teach me how to revive mine." The compliment alone will stir that neighbor to help you, because he or she will be excited that someone else sees the beauty in all that work they put in daily.

We have not...because we ask not!

IMPRISONED BY THE MIND

If we aren't careful, our minds can be the very institution that incarcerates us for life. But it is your right to be bound and shackled by your own mind, because it is yours. What I have a problem with is when a person starts thinking they know what I need, how I or anyone else should live, what is too good for me. It really isn't your business. Maybe what's good enough for you isn't good enough for me. I have different standards. It is impossible for you to want the best that God wants for me. So, decide for yourself, I *will not* allow you to decide for me. I reached the age of accountability ages ago. What can you do for me locked in your mind anyway?

SUICIDE

Full tank of gas to take me to hell ✔
Thirty days supply of OxyContin ✔
A bottle of gin to wash it down ✔
My 38 "not-so-special" in case I punk out ✔

Driving along to nowhere, I loosened my tie.
I turned off my phone. In about half an hour Sondra would call wondering why I wasn't home for dinner yet. I couldn't face my pregnant wife. She's beautiful, ripe, swollen with my seed. I couldn't face my six-year-old twin boys. Today had been her appointment to find out the sex of the baby. I know she was excited about telling me the results. She's probably called already, but I was busy. Busy getting fired. The merger fell through. My cut—two hundred and fifty grand—swirled down the drain in front of me, slowly, so I could see what it looked like from all angles. Apart from that, stocks fell as a result, so all I did today was lose. How could I tell my pregnant wife, my children, that I'd gambled with fate? We'd already planned that cut—allotted it to college funds, a home and savings. My wife doesn't know anything about hard life, she'd done everything by the book, came from good stock, studied and excelled and worked her fingers to the bone. I promised her that I could give her the life she was accustomed to. I asked her to trade her Armani suits and Red Bottoms for aprons and a hot stove, and she loved me enough to do it. She loved me enough to support my dreams, to wait a

while, to remove her brain and put it into a box—for me. I love her madly, and I owe her greatly.

I had decided to take my life. Earlier I wrote her a note, telling her how sorry I was about everything. I apologized to her for breaking her heart, disappointing her. I figured when they find me bloated and stinking, they'd give her the note—it bore her name—she is my next of kin.

That car just sped by me doing top speed. I wondered what was the hurry. The blur of the vehicle looked vaguely familiar. Anyway, later for him or her, I was on a mission. About three miles up the road I saw a cloud of dust. That fast vehicle had come to a mangled stop. It was down a ravine, hugging a tree—driver's side. First thought was call for help. Call 911. Ding, ding, ding. My phone went wild with message alerts. I had two missed messages. One from Sondra, one from my boss—former boss that is.

After about seven minutes I heard the wail of sirens and help arrived. From that vaguely familiar rubble came the unconscious body of my former boss's son. I stood there in amazement.

Doing what I'd normally do in distress, I longed to hear Sondra's voice. Listening to her message it said, (screaming/crying/giggling/shouting) "Tyrell, I love you. Our baby is going to be a girl. I'm so excited! When I left the doctor I had a craving for fried chicken so I stopped at the deli and got me some. While I waited I bought a scratch ticket for a dollar, just so I could pass the time. Baby? We won a million dollars. (more screaming) You need to call me!" I was in shock. I honestly should be dead were it not for the accident.

Message two from my former boss: "Tyrell, I may have been a bit hasty today. I may have something else in mind that I need you to oversee. Please report to work same time as usual tomorrow." Hmmm...I watched them board the young man and off they went with him. I only told them that I came up on the accident scene. From the looks of things, if Scott lives, he'll lose both legs. Someone had lost much more than I did today. That hit me like a ton of bricks. I will be there for my boss. I really didn't deserve all I was blessed with. Just because I couldn't face the music, I had made a decision to end my life.

Turning on the radio, I heard the voice of a preacher saying, "Even when we feel we are all alone God is with us." I shifted in my seat uncomfortably and looked around within the cabin of my car. I knew right then and there that God was with me. He took me to the bottom in less than a day, then taught me that somebody out there has it worse than me. Showed me all that I could gain if I'd just trust him. Right there on the side of the road I cried out to God, I asked him to forgive me of my sins. Told him to guide me in ways that would make me a better husband, father, person in general. Asked him to come into my heart. Then I did something I've never done before: I littered. I emptied that bottle of pills and that bottle of gin and threw them as far as my arm would allow me.

Then I called my beautiful wife, who always has been my walking, breathing miracle. She'd always managed to shift things, just by being herself. My ace of spades. The minute she heard my voice, she started screaming and giggling. I started chortling too. "I'm coming home, baby. I am coming home".

~

I PRAY FOR YOU

Friends—just know that you are on my "friends" list for a reason; it's no mistake. Know that I love you all and I am praying for you, whether you put emphasis on the power of prayer or not. Sometimes it's the prayers of those who know the power of it that sustains us. Many times it is someone lifting your name up to God that is the barrier between you and the devil's snare. Whenever any of your names come to mind, I speak it and ask that you be covered and protected. I ask that the covering be extended to your family—that they get the overflow. Something tells me that many of you are going through some things. It's going to be okay. Response to pain has always been a good sign in medicine. Whenever I touched an area on a person and they cried out, that made me feel good because I knew that area was alive. Much like us in our everyday lives. When you feel the pain of the situation, just look up and say, "Thank you, Lord." Thank him for the ability to actually feel the pain, push through it and come out having grown from it. It is going to be okay! Somebody somewhere is praying for you!

~

AIN'T NOBODY LIKE JESUS!

I don't know if you know it yet, but ain't nobody like Jesus!

My Affair with Haiku

LEAVES

Leaves vibrant green life
How long will you
challenge time
Fallen on the ground

HEARTBEAT

My heart beats for you
Sometimes it chases itself
When you are around

WATER

Flowing cool and fresh
Delicious you taste always
Quench my every thirst

SUN

Bright and beautiful
You give me the energy
When I need it most

GOD

Mysterious One
Ever present at all times
Always at our side

POETRY

Mysteriously
Poetry takes me places
My ardent lover

LOVE?!

I was not prepared
This thing called love... where
were you?
Where did you come from?

UGH!

Persistently you
Chip away at my defense
When will you give up?

SCENT

The smell of you is
Intoxicating to me…
Alluring to me…

TOUCH

Put your hand on me
Never let me go until
Death stares in your face

DESIRE

I could hardly wait
To get you alone with me
I hunger for you

RAINY DAYS

I love rainy days
Comfort falling from the skies
Waking up my soul

PETS

Pets are such a joy
Making our lives so special
Healing fur-ever

SEIZE THE DAY

Tick-tock. Tick-tock. Tick.
The sound of time passing by
It will not return!

DREAMS

Your dreams will chase you
Driving you mad with unease
Stand still and listen.

RAIN

Rain does something to my senses
As I hear it fall attention stealing
Each drop dances on my nerves
Exciting my thoughts to faraway places
It calls me to run outside and dance in it
To let it wash away the world
The smell of new earth entices
In ways that make me giggle as it falls
At other times it makes me want to cuddle
Beneath a blanket soft and powder-scented
Pitter-patter on the roof it cleanses
Washing things away I'd hate to see
Sometimes gently, sometimes forcefully
Perfect showers each time at any hour
I am madly in love with the rain
I know it is madly in love with me

～

SNOW

Beautiful white snow
Purifies all it touches
Amazing beauty
Your season compares to none
Always stunned by you I am

～

THE WIND

I wanted to feel you
So I rushed out the door
Leaving my shoes and clothing behind, my soles touched the dewy grass
A cool kiss against them for my memory
You rewarded me with the lively smell as the blades were crushed beneath my eager feet.
Here you are, great wind, dancing against my naked flesh. Filling my lungs.
Goosebumps rise in praise of you.
You come from the four directions, whispering to me.
Urging me to fly if I want to. But no…not yet…
I am content to take you as a lover
To allow you to touch every part of me, blow through my hair
Telling me your secrets, while I tell you mine
Brushing against my side, you remind me of how alive I am
Far off I hear parts of you engaged in conversation—two distinct howling tones.
Indecipherable yet sound!

I thank you great wind, we will meet again.
Until then, deliver my dreams as you always have.
My time with you has been intoxicating.

∾

SHHH...

Much is heard in silence.
Become one with nature and sit in stillness.
Listen to your heartbeat as it pumps blood through your veins.
Close your eyes and feel your lungs expand; listen to them filter and work the air that you need. Externally, you hear the rustling of the leaves and branches as they sway in their very own way.
Listen to the wind as it brings new life to your thoughts
One by one in stillness arrange your thoughts as you see fit, listen to them state their case, debate with them, come to a conclusion.
Out here you can hear them
Take back your power by slowing them down
You decide what to think next
Trace your palms over the soft grass and feel them bring to life every fiber of your being
Feel the coolness against your skin
In this moment recognize how treasured you are
Just how blessed you are to be alive
Pay homage mentally to those who walked right where you are seated before, never to return. You are significant
You are worthy of all that is good
You are whole
You are growing
Nothing else matters in this moment but YOU
When you arise your spirit will be refreshed
Shhh...
In silence you can almost hear the grass grow.

THANK YOU!

Lord, today I just want to say THANK YOU! Sitting here just now, I came to the realization that every professional and educational decision I've made has been guided. Every step I have taken has prepared me for this moment, and I just thank my Jesus. Thank you for seeing about your girl. Please stay with me always. This journey is so interesting with its crossroads, bends, rains I've had to shelter from and potholes that kept me back from destruction. I thank you for all the STOP signs, patience during train crossings, YIELD signs and speed limits. Thank you for carrying me when I was weary. Thank you Lord! THANK YOU!

GOD CALLED YOU!

Walk sturdy! Have no fear!
It's no mistake you are standing here
He is certain of YOU
Empowered to do what he's called YOU to do

Leave all failure behind
He has given you a sound mind
YOU will shock them—I know
God has already given the go

Just trust him! Have faith!
He says, "No longer will you wait"
Be prayerful. He'll guide
Forever standing by your side

He made YOU like him
Knowing this, YOU are sure to win
Just do it, you have help
GOD called you! Just say YES!

∽

BUCKET LIST!

Well, for those of you who know me, you know I have a bucket list. I've managed to check off quite a few things. At seventeen, I made a list, and as life changes, I've added things and checked things off. I wanted to visit Italy and Greece and was blessed to spend a month over there. Bungee jumping—did it; it was fun. Getting on challenging roller coasters—did that! I still seek them out. I traveled to many of my Caribbean islands—loved them all—especially Dominica. Yes, I love Dominica more than Antigua (where I am from). I wanted to see South America and was blessed to tour there.

I was curious about cruising, because when I was a little girl, I thought only rich people could cruise. Well, I'm still not rich *yet*, but I've managed to go on six cruises; so far I've tried three lines, and my favorite is Princess because I like to be pampered, I enjoy luxury and appreciate good food; I like to cook and am good at it but enjoy being fed. I've worked hard to be able to check off my items: long hours, strange shifts with a few odd individuals!

Road trips—I've done a few and like them, especially if it's some-place new. I get a thrill out of pulling into a rest stop and leaving knowing I've been there. Currently I'm writing my book—publish-ing will be another check on that list. I must see Paris, suggested by a high school teacher I ran into a few years ago. I was always curious, but she heightened my curiosity with her exciting report. I'd like to spend some time at a ski lodge. Yes, I must ski! Even if my leg is in a cast afterwards, that's fine! I just MUST do it; it looks like fun.

This bucket list of mine was first scribbled on paper, then it's been on computers, and today it's on my iPad. Through it all, God has been with me; he made me and knows the things I like to do. He knows I like to take chances, so He has a time with this particular child of His. I've never been a timid person who is afraid to explore. I'm the type to try something, give it my best and not harp over it if it doesn't work out. I believe we should live life to the fullest, eat well, travel, LOVE like it's the very last time you are seeing somebody and forgive. Forgiveness cleanses the spirit and allows us to move on. I've never believed in mourning a lost love—nobody died—just move on and say to yourself, that person is no longer necessary for your journey. The only people I will ever lose sleep over are my parents.

Today I am just thankful to God and wanted to share it. Not everybody will agree with me on the way I live my life, but that's fine. So hold whatever opinion you want, it matters not. Today I am just thankful! And I ask the Lord to continue to guide and carry my family. Without him I am nothing. Don't just exist...put actual effort into living and ENJOY YOUR LIFE!

ANSWERED PRAYER

It is really done. It's completed. Over. Ended. Lord, thank you for that quick turnaround. Thank you for going before me. Thank you for answered prayer. Glory Hallelujah!

NEVER GIVE UP

Never give up, you are almost through
There's just a little more work to do
God is with you at your side
Your ever-present, helpful guide

He'll pick you up if you should fall
He'll stay with you through it all
I know you are tired, precious friend
But he promises to stay until the end

Rest if you must, don't feel ashamed
Though you have cried more tears remain
Each is counted and written down
So smile through your journey, don't wear a frown

The finish line is just up ahead
Keep on pushing your steps are led
Your path was cleared before the start
Your direction was scripted on your heart

Ignore the noise when it should come
Little do you know, "You're almost done"
Angels surround you, look around, look up
Whatever you do just never give up.

*Though thy beginning was small,
yet thy latter end should greatly increase* (Job 8:7).

THE END…
Nah, scratch that…
JUST THE BEGINNING :)

About the Author

Renna Roberts-Gore describes poetry as "the walls of the soul" and proves herself as an emotional nudist who encourages others to share their stories. With a background in behavioral science, Renna is a certified life coach, a veteran of the US Navy, and a retired EMT after eighteen years. She has a deep understanding of the many hardships in life as well as the greatness that can come out of those experiences.

Along with sharing her voice through writing, Renna enjoys reading and servicing her community in Orlando, Florida, where she volunteers as a hearing officer with the youth division. Renna is a true believer of crossing off your bucket list and has traveled to over thirty countries—so far. She is an excellent cook and especially enjoys making multi-cultural meals for her husband, Winston, and son, Kyle.

As an avid animal lover and owner of two rescue dogs, Bailey and Midnight, Renna will be donating proceeds from the sale of her book towards the care, treatment, and housing of animals in the state of Florida.

To learn more, visit www.RennaGore.com.

WE WANT TO HEAR FROM YOU!!!

If this book has made a difference in your life
Renna would be delighted to hear about it.
Leave a review on Amazon.com!

BOOK RENNA TO SPEAK AT YOUR NEXT EVENT!
Send an email to: booking@publishyourgift.com

LEARN MORE ABOUT RENNA AT:
www.RennaGore.com

CPSIA information can be obtained
at www.ICGtesting.com
Printed in the USA
LVOW04s0906210516
489316LV00008B/32/P